Poland is a hospitable and friendly country
with countless reminders of its great past,
a picturesque landscape and outstanding
natural riches. Its folk tradition survives
inmany places. Together, these factors
confirm Poland's status as an interesting
and attractive land for tourists.

POLAND

1/2/2013

To Kasterboum Family
with affection
♡ Margaret
Enjoy !!

POLAND

 Wydawnictwo PARMA® PRESS

Illustration on the cover: Warsaw, the Palace in Wilanów.
Illustration on the title pages: The landscape of the Kielce region.

Photos: CHRISTIAN PARMA

Text and layout: BOGNA PARMA

Translation: JAMES RICHARDS

Map: MARIUSZ SZELEREWICZ

Publisher: Wydawnictwo PARMA PRESS
                    05-270 Marki, al. Józefa Piłsudskiego 189 b
                    + 48 22/ 781 16 48, 781 16 49, 781 12 31
                    e-mail: wydawnictwo@parmapress.com.pl
                    www.parmapress.com.pl

ISBN 978-83-7777-033-7

Poland lies at the geometric centre of Europe. In the north it is washed by the waves of the Baltic Sea, while in the south it is also limited by a natural boundary in the form of the Western Carpathians, which extend from the Bieszczady Mountains, via the Tatras and Beskids, as far as the Sudetic Mountains and the picturesque Karkonosze. In the east, Poland ends at the River Bug, while in the west it is the Oder and Nysa Łużycka that form the border. Though very largely a land of plains, an average altitude of 174 m a.s.l. conceals the fact that this is a far from monotonous landscape.

The Polish coast tends to be a flat one of wide sandy beaches, though occasional cliffs rise up here and there, as at Gdynia Orłowo. There are also extensive coastal dunes, for example in the Łeba area.

As we move south from the Baltic we encounter a zone of extensive lakelands, including the Pomeranian Lakeland and the Mazurian Lake District. The landscape here is predominantly post-glacial, with a wealth of what are Poland's largest and deepest lakes set amongst morainic elevations covered in forest. Perhaps the least diverse countryside, though no less charming for that, is the plainland heart of Poland, formed by the Mazowsze (Mazovia), Wielkopolska and Silesian regions.

Still further south, the land rises steadily: first in a belt formed by the Lublin, Małopolska and Silesian Uplands. An interesting area within the second of these is that of the Kraków-Wieluń Upland with its characteristic limestone rocks, a wealth of caves and picturesque gorges. A major tourist attraction here is the Trail of the Eagles' Nests (Szlak Orlich Gniazd) with its ruins of Mediaeval castles and fortresses.

The mountains proper arise just a little further to the south. In the south-eastern corner, the gentleness of the Bieszczady Mountain peaks belies the nature of what is a heavily-forested and truly wild land. Moving west along the southern border we reach the Tatras, Poland's youngest and highest mountains, having passed through the Pieniny Range, with its famous gorge of the Dunajec. Still further to the west the highlands continue with the Silesian Beskids. The Sudetic Mountains begin at the so-called Moravian Gate. The most interesting range within t hem are the Karkonosze Mountains, where the rock formations take on the strangest of shapes.

The country's biggest river, the Vistula, flows from south to north. It is one of the last big rivers in Europe to remain very largely unregulated.

The name Poland itself relates back to the Polanie tribe, a people inhabiting what is now Wielkopolska in the Early Middle Ages.

The year 966 saw Poland's conversion to Christianity with the baptism of Mieszko I, regarded as the first leader of Poland. He was succeeded by his son Bolesław the Brave, who was able to found a strong and stable state with its capital in Gniezno. His death was followed by a collapse of authority made worse by the division of the country into districts from 1138 on – a consequence of provisions in the last will and testament of Bolesław III "Wrymouth". The reunification of the country had to wait until 1320, a year which marked a highpoint in the 27-year reign of Władysław I ("the Short").

In the mid 14th century the Polish throne was occupied by King Kazimierz III ("the Great"), who was able to strengthen the country in terms of its internal security and its economic prowess. It was he who founded Poland's first university (later known as the Jagiellonian) in Kraków, and he who has gone down in history as the ruler who "found Poland in wood and left her in brick". At the same time, however, the growing strength of the Order of the Teutonic Knights left Poland cut off from its access to the Baltic, while threatening the very existence of Lithuania. This state of affairs led to the Polish-Lithuanian Union of 1385 and the subsequent rule of the Jagiellonian Dynasty. This made a promising start when a united army under Władysław Jagiełło defeated the Teutonic Knights at the Battle of Grunwald in 1410.

Economic growth continued and the power of the nobility increased. By the 16th century, Poland was something of a superpower, being Europe's largest state, and one of its richest. This was the so-called Golden Age in the country's history. It was also at this time that Zygmunt III Vasa transferred his capital from Kraków to Warsaw.

Later decades were less happy for Poland. A Cossack revolt broke out in the Ukraine, while the Swedish invasion or "Deluge" brought territorial losses and economic ruin. The country's internal stability was lost and a central authority was often lacking.

In seeking to restore statehood from all this chaos, Poles commenced with reforms in education, the economy and defence. The crowning of these efforts came with the adoption in 1791 of the very progressive Constitution of May 3rd, Europe's first, and only the second in the world after that of the United States.

Alas, this national reconciliation came too late. The three partitions of 1772, 1792 and 1795 saw Poland divided between the Russian, Prussian and Austrian Empires. The result was the country's disappearance from the map of Europe for 123 years.

Poles launched uprisings again and again, but it was only in 1918 – as the disasters of the First World War combined with revolution to bring the three partitioning powers low – that Poland regained its statehood. Józef Piłsudski became leader of the reborn country on November 11th 1918 – recognised to this day as Polish Independence Day.

The freedom was shortlived. Hitler's Nazis fell upon Poland on September 1st 1939, thereby precipitating the Second World War. Polish soldiers fought on all fronts, but the War's end in 1945 did not resolve the matter of independence. Rather, the Yalta Conference left Poland firmly under the influence of the Soviet Union.

Many years of steadfast national opposition to an imposed system were ultimately to lead to the establishment of the Solidarity trade union in 1980.

The mass opposition to the communist authorities it was able to mobilise ensured that it was only a matter of time before the regime began to give way. The breakthrough year was 1989, when representatives of the opposition and the then authorities met at the "Round Table" to discuss the gradual democratisation of the country. Solidarity's leader, Lech Wałęsa, was ultimately to become President. The events begun in Poland had meanwhile exerted a far-from-trivial influence on the political situation throughout Europe.

The return of national sovereignty led Poland to seek NATO membership, which it achieved on March 12th 1999. In turn, economic development and political will allowed the country to accede to the European Union on May 1st 2004.

The Poland of today covers around 312,500 km^2. It is bounded in the West by Germany, in the south by the Czech Republic and Slovakia, and in the east by Ukraine, Belarus, Lithuania and Russia. The emblem of Poland is a crowned white eagle facing to its right, with golden beak and talons, in a red field upon a rectangular shield.

Poland has c. 40 million inhabitants, mainly of Polish nationality and very largely Roman Catholic. Their faith is sustained by the first Polish Pope in history, His Holiness John Paul II. Poles do not forget the martyrs of the past, and there are many monuments and places of national remembrance. The largest of all is at Oświęcim – site of the former Auschwitz Concentration Camp.

Poland has a wealth of UNESCO World Heritage Sites, including Old Kraków, the town of Zamość with its Renaissance architecture, the Wieliczka Salt Mine and the Białowieża National Park (which is also a Biosphere Reserve).

Poland is a hospitable and friendly country with countless reminders of its great past, a picturesque landscape and outstanding natural riches. Its folk tradition survives in many places. Together, these factors confirm Poland's status as an interesting and attractive land for tourists.

Superlatives

The largest city:	– Warsaw, the capital of Poland, on the Vistula, with c.1.7 million inhabitants and an area of around 500 km²;
The largest voivodship (province):	– Mazowieckie (formerly Mazovia, capital Warsaw), which today covers c. 36,000 km and has more than 5 million inhabitants;
The longest river:	– the Vistula (Wisła), which has its source beneath Barania Góra in the Silesian Beskid Range and runs 1068 km to empty into the Baltic in the Gulf of Gdańsk;
The highest peak:	– the north-western summit of Rysy at 2499 m, within the High Tatras;
The lowest point:	– an altitude of 1.8 m a.s.l. in the Żuławy Wiślane (Vistula Delta) area;
The deepest lowland lake:	– the ribbon-lake Lake Hańcza in the Mazurian Lakeland, with a maximum depth of 108 m;
The deepest mountain lake:	– the cirque-lake known as Wielki Staw Polski (the Great Polish Tarn), one of the lakes in The Valley of the Five Polish Tarns (Dolina Pięciu Stawów Polskich) within the High Tatras – maximum depth 79.3 m;
The largest lake:	– the morainic lake Lake Śniardwy covering 109.7 km² in the Mazurian Lakeland;
The largest National Park:	– the Biebrza (Biebrzański) National Park, protecting 59,223 ha of fen and bogland unique anywhere in Europe;
The largest church:	– Poland's largest church is at Licheń Stary near Konin, a Sanctuary of Our Lady and Basilica enclosing a volume of no less than 300,700 m³;
The largest castle:	– the Gothic-style 13th-15th century fortress of the Teutonic Knights at Malbork, an outstanding example of a Mediaeval fortification;
The best-known sanctuary:	– that of the Virgin Mary with its miraculous likeness of the Black Madonna, on the Jasna Góra hill in Częstochowa;
The longest market square:	– the 400-metre cobbled example in Pułtusk;
The oldest place of learning:	– Kraków's Jagiellonian University established in 1364;
The oldest town:	– Kalisz, referred to as Kalisia in the 2nd century AD by Ptolemy;
The most unusual residence:	– the Krzyżtopór castle which boasted – before its destruction – as many windows as there are days in the year, as many rooms as there are weeks, as many halls as there are months and as many towers as there are quarters. The ceiling of one hall formed the floor of an aquarium with fish;
The oldest entry in Polish:	– "Day, ut ia pobrusa, a ti poziwai" ("Give it here, I'll turn it and you rest"), in the "Book of Henryków" from 1270

GDAŃSK is an old Hanseatic town whose major development occurred
in the 15th to 18th centuries, when it was the wealthiest city in the Republic.
To be seen here is a panorama of the historical Główne Miasto
(Main Town), with the Mariacki (St. Mary's) Church from
the 14th-15th centuries – the largest place of worship in Poland.

GDAŃSK. A view of the Lonq Quayside by the Motława with its Mediaeval hoist.

GDAŃSK is a historic port city and one of the most outstanding complexes of heritage buildings in Poland. Here we see Długi Targ with the Gothic-style Town Hall of the Main Town and its 82-metre tower.

GDAŃSK. The Neptune Fountain on Długi Targ (the Long Market).

GDAŃSK. The richly-decorated portal of one of the tenement houses on Długi Targ.

GDYNIA ORŁOWO with its elevated cliff coastline so unsual for Poland.

GDYNIA is a large commercial, military and passenger port and a centre of the maritime economy. The three-masted sailing ship "Dar Młodzieży" ("Gift of Youth"), training vessel of the Merchant Navy Academy, at its moorings by the South Pier.

SOPOT is the lying between Gdańsk and Gdynia and forming with the so-colled Trójmiasto ("Tri-City"). An attractive tourist centre, it boasts sea bathing, health-resort facilities and a 19th-centry pier.

TRZĘSACZ, where we visit the famous clifftop ruins of a 14th-century church "claimed by the sea".

THE BALTIC SEA.
The seashore in Dziwnów.

*MIĘDZYZDROJE
is a fashionable place
of seaside recreation.*

*MIĘDZYZDROJE is situated
on Wolin Island, with
its fishing boats.*

SZCZECIN is a large commercial port and centre of shipbuilding on the Szczecin Lagoon. Its Old Market Square boasts a 15th-century Town Hall.

SZCZECIN began as a Lusatian settlement 2500 years ago. It was part of the Hanseatic League from the 13th century onwards. Wały Chrobrego is a leading thoroughfare along the Oder, lined by monumental buildings from the early 20th century.

SZCZECIN. The Gothic-style Cathedral of St. James the Apostle was rebuilt as recently as in the years 1971-1975, having been destroyed during the Second World War.

SZCZECIN. The ornate doorway of a tenement house on Grodzka Street.

SZCZECIN. The Renaissance castle of the Dukes of Pomerania is multi-winged, with two courtyards. It was rebuilt post-1945.

STARGARD SZCZECIŃSKI is a Western Pomeranian town with a mediaeval architectural plan.

The two-towered Church of the Blessed Virgin Mary dates back to the Gothic period.

KAMIEŃ POMORSKI is a health resort on the Kamień Lagoon, a few kilometres inland from the sea.

This old fortified port town boasts a late-Gothic Town Hall from the 15th-16th centuries.

KAMIEŃ POMORSKI. A section of the Baroque-style pulpit in the Gothic Cathedral of the Blessed Virgin Mary and St. John the Baptist.

DRAWSKO POMORSKIE is a town in the Drawskie Lakeland.

Here a baked-brick bestiary adorns the side entrance of a 14th-century church.

BISKUPIN. The reconstruction of an early Slav settlement from the Hallstatt period. 25 centuries ago this settlement had about 1000 inhabitants!

OSTRÓW LEDNICKI. An island with an archaeological reserve, regional open-air museum and ruins of a 10th-century ducal castle.

GNIEZNO. In the 8th century, this was the main walled town of the Polanie tribe.
The 14th-15th century Gothic Cathedral of the Assumption of the Virgin Mary and St. Adalbert was the place of coronation of five Polish Kings.

GNIEZNO. This Monument to King Bolesław Chrobry dates back to 1925, but was only reconstructed in 1985.

POZNAŃ – situated on the Warta –
is the historic capital of the Wielkopolska region.
The Cathedral of Saints Peter and Paul on Ostrów
Tumski island had its origins in the 10th century.

POZNAŃ. Bronze likenesses of two members
of Poland's Piast dynasty: Mieszko I and Bolesław
Chrobry ("the Brave"), in the Golden Chapel
at Poznań Cathedral.

POZNAŃ. A Late-Gothic polyptych
on the Cathedral's main altar.

POZNAŃ. The Old Market Square with
its interestingly arcaded Town Hall.

POZNAŃ. The goats of the Town Hall
clock engage in butting contests daily
at midday.

POZNAŃ. A small sculpture
of a female settler from Bamberg, 1914.

RYDZYNA is a small historic town in the Wielkopolska region.
Standing in an extensive landscaped park, the Baroque palace
of the Sułkowski family dates back to the 17th and 18th centuries.

RYDZYNA. The Rococo figure of the Holy Trinity
in the middle of the Market Square.

WSCHOWA in Wielkopolska provides fine examples of Baroque town buildings. Here we see the Neo-Gothic Town Hall on the Market Square.

DĘBOWA ŁĘKA.
A stork's nest –
a typically Polish view.

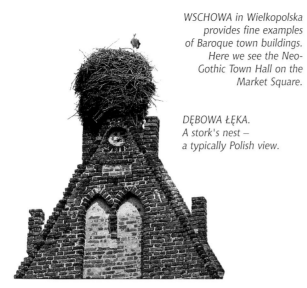

KÓRNIK. The original castle dating back to 1426 was extensively remodelled in the English neo-Gothic style in the 19th century.

GOSTYŃ, with its Philippinian monastery complex, Sanctuary to the Virgin Mary and 17th-century church, and well in the viridarium.

BOSZKOWO is a place of rest and recreation in the Leszno Lakeland.

KALISZ is a town whose history stretches back to Roman times. Here the Baroque Collegiate Church of the Assumption of the Blessed Virgin Mary and St. Joseph.

GOŁUCHÓW boasts a 16th-century Renaissance castle remodelled in the style of the French Renaissance in the 19th century and set in picturesque English-style parkland.

WROCŁAW, the capital of Lower Silesia, is a historic city on the Oder which began life as a Slav settlement in the first millennium. Standing on Ostrów Tumski island is the Gothic Cathedral dedicated to St. John the Baptist.

WROCŁAW. The Racławicka panorama is a 19th century painted battle scene with a circumference of 114 m and a height of 15 m. It represents the work of a great many artists under the direction of Wojciech Kossak and Jan Styka.

WROCŁAW. The characteristic Gothic Town Hall, from the 14th-15th centuries, features richly-decorated facades and a 66-metre tower.

WROCŁAW. Figures representing justice stand guard by the entrance to the Town Hall. The armed servant of a village chief is a copy of a 15th -century sculpture that now lies in pieces in a museum.

GÓRY SOWIE (the Owl Mountains) are a well-forested range built of Pre-Cambrian shales forming part of the Central Sudetic Mountains.

The KARKONOSZE form a range within the Sudetic Mountains that peak at the 1602 m Śnieżka massif. In winter they take on a particular beauty.

CIEPLICE ŚLĄSKIE ZDRÓJ is a spa town now within the city limits of Jelenia Góra. Here an interior of the Late Baroque palace of the Schaffgotsch family.

KARPACZ is a holiday resort at the foot of Śnieżka mountain. The Wang church was brought here from Norway in the 19th century, though its origins go back six centuries before that.

JASKINIA NIEDŹWIEDZIA (the Bear Cave) lies at the foot of Śnieżnik and is richer in dripstone features than any other cave in Poland.

KSIĄŻ boasts the imposing 16th-century castle of the Hochbergs – the largest castle in Lower Silesia. It has often been remodelled, most notably in the Baroque style in the 18th century.

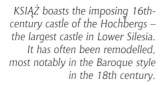

KSIĄŻ. The well in the Castle's "Black Courtyard".

KSIĄŻ – the castle features nearly 400 rooms in various architectural styles.

The Baroque ballroom from the first half of the 18th century is known as the Maximilian Room.

WAMBIERZYCE is a well-known place of pilgrimage whose Sanctuary to the Virgin Mary led it to be called the Silesian Jerusalem. The monumental 56-step staircase leads to the late Baroque Church of the Visitation.

The RIVER ODER is Lower Silesia's biggest. Here a barge navigates the channels of the Oder in Brzeg.

BRZEG. 17th-century scratchwork decoration on the elevation of the Town Hall courtyard.

BRZEG boasts an Old Town from the Middle Ages laid out in a grid pattern. The Town Hall is the most beautiful Renaissance example anywhere in Silesia.

BRZEG. Here Duke Jerzy II and his wife Barbara of Brandenburg are sculpted into the facade of the gatehouse building of the 16th-century Renaissance-style castle.

MAŁUJOWICE. The Church interior is adorned by Mediaeval wall painting.

MAŁUJOWICE is a locality along the trail of Brzeg polychromy. Here a fragment of the wall painting in the presbytery of the Gothic Church of St. James the Apostle.

MOSZNA, near Opole, features an eclectic-style castle from the late 19th century.

OPOLE. The Młynówka,
one of the several branches
of the Oder that have
led locals to use the term
"the Opole Venice".

OPOLE – a historic town on the Oder
– is the capital of Opole Silesia.
This view of a fragment of the southern
side of the market square features
16th- century tenement houses and the
tower of the Church of the Holy Trinity.

OPOLE. The Millennium
Amphitheatre dating back
to 1963 draws fans annually
to Festivals of Polish Song.

BESKID ŚLĄSKI is the furthest west of the Beskid ranges and is well-frequented by tourists. This view from Czantoria shows why.

ŻYWIEC has enjoyed town rights since 1420. It is above all known for its brewery, founded 1856. Here, the arcaded Renaissance courtyard of the Old Castle.

CIESZYN, on the Olza, is the capital of Cieszyn Silesia. This photograph shows one facade of the market square with 18th-century arcaded tenement houses.

A girl from the "Śląsk" song and dance ensemble in the traditional townwear of the region known as Cieszyn (Teschen) Silesia.

CIESZYN. The 11th-century Romanesque-style rotunda dedicated to St. Nicholas is situated on the tree-covered Castle Hill. It takes the form of a circle of diameter 6.4 m.

*KATOWICE is Upper Silesia's main city.
This historic building in the centre.*

*KATOWICE. This plaque honours the memory
of the fallen miners at the "Wujek" coalmine;
a symbol of Poles' resistance to the period
of Martial Law introduced in 1981.*

*KATOWICE also boasts a three-winged
Monument to the Silesian Uprisings
of 1919, 1920 and 1921 which was
unveiled in 1967.*

*THE UPPER
INDUSTRIAL DISTRICT,
includes the Katowice
Steelworks, which
is actually just
beyond Silesia in the
Zagłębie region.*

BRZEZINKA (Birkenau) held a sub-camp of the parent Oświęcim (Auschwitz) Concentration Camp. This is a characteristic railway loading platform.

BRZEZINKA. Moving traces of people's existence in the death camp – wall illustrations presenting the gehenna of camp life.

OŚWIĘCIM, still better known to millions by its German name of Auschwitz, remains a symbol of the Holocaust. The site of the former Nazi concentration camp is today a museum recalling the full horror of what happened here.

CZĘSTOCHOWA is famed for the Paulite Monastery on
the Jasna Góra hill, a place of pilgrimage for millions
and centre of the cult of the Częstochowa Madonna.
To be seen here are the basilica and Lubomirski Gate.

CZĘSTOCHOWA. The miraculous likeness of the Black Madonna of Jasna Góra is an icon which has attracted millions of pilgrims down the centuries. For most of the time it is partially hidden behind a cover representing a uniqe triumph of the jeweller's art.

CZĘSTOCHOWA and the Baroque interior of the Basilica of the Assumption of the Virgin Mary.

SIERADZ. Here the Sieradzanię ensemble present the śmigus-dyngus folk custom entailing the soaking of all-comers with water on Easter Monday.

TUM, near Łęczyca, boasts a stone Romanesque collegiate church from the 12th century, with its gloomy, severe interior.

ŁĘCZYCA was once apparently ruled over by the devil Boruta. To be seen here is the restored 14th-century castle.

UNIEJÓW. The remodelled castle dating back to the 14th century was once the residence of Bishops.

ŁĘCZYCA. Carvings of devil in the castle courtyard.

45

ŁÓDŹ is a city whose flowering came in the mid 19th century, as the textile industry developed. In this photo, Freedom Square (Plac Wolności) with its Monument to Tadeusz Kościuszko, Church of the Holy Spirit and former Town Hall from the 19th century.

ŁÓDŹ. Piotrkowska Street, the city's main thoroughfare, stretches for 4 km, and is regarded as Europe's longest commercial street.

ŁÓDŹ is rich in old Secession-style architecture. This is the Neo-Baroque palace complex of the Poznański family, with its rich eclectic-style facade.

ŁÓDŹ. An ornamental detail on the facade of the Poznański's Palace.

LICHEŃ STARY is a famous place of pilgrimage not far from Konin, with a Sanctuary to the Virgin Mary kept by Marian priests containing the miraculous likeness of the Licheń Mother of God.

LICHEŃ STARY – on the Sanctuary site there are many buildings, chapels and other places devoted to national remembrance. The characteristic "Golgotha" is a source of great interest.

TORUŃ. The view from the Town Hall tower towards the Gothic-style Church of the Blessed Virgin Mary.

TORUŃ. This heritage-rich old town was once within the Hanseatic League. Here we see the monument to the city's most famous son, Nicholas Copernicus, against the background of the Gothic-style Town Hall, as well as the 18th-century Church of the Holy Spirit.

TORUŃ.
The fountain
with the statuette
of a bargee.

CIECHOCINEK has been a place to spa waters since the 19th century. Here, the wooden building in which salty vapours can be inhaled, along with the flower clock in the Park.

BYDGOSZCZ, with the Statue of the Archer.

BYDGOSZCZ, on the Brda, was a centre trading ingrain and salt in the 15th and 16th centuries. This photo shows Gdańska Street with the Pod Orlem ("Sign of the Eagle") Hotel.

CHEŁMNO is a picturesque town that retains its Mediaeval town plan. Standing on a market square covering more than 1.5 ha, the 14th-century Town Hall was remodelled in the Mannerist style two centuries later.

GOLUB-DOBRZYŃ boasts a 14th-century castle remodelled in Renaissance style in the 1600s. Each year, this plays host to tournaments of jousting and other chivalrous skills.

GNIEW. Overlooking the Vistula is a 14th-century castle of the Teutonic Knights that was built in the shape of a regular square.

KWIDZYN has a monumental Gothic castle of brick, together with a fortified cathedral built by the Order of the Teutonic Knights.

MALBORK – another town of the Teutonic Knights
– is situated on the bank of the Nogat.
The castle, which was the seat of the Order's Grand
Masters, dates back to the 13th-15th centuries, and is one
of the finest surviving examples of a Mediaeval fortress.

GRUNWALD. The Monument to the Victors of the Battle of Grunwald commemorates the defeat of the Teutonic Knights here in 1410.

GRUNWALD. Latter-day knights meet on the battlefield every year in order to recreate the famous victory.

IŁAWA is a centre of waterborne recreation and tourism by Lake Jeziorak. This is a pier built out into the water for anglers.

MORĄG is a town founded in 1327 by the Teutonic Knights. Pictured here is the remodelled Gothic-style Town Hall.

MIŁOMŁYN. A sluice on the Ostróda-Elbląg Canal.

OLSZTYN on the River Łyna and within the Olsztyn Lakeland. This reconstructed 14th-century castle was that of the Varmia Chapter.

OLSZTYN. Freedom Square (Plac Wolności) with its early 20th-century Town Hall built in a style that recalls the Baroque and Renaissance periods.

OLSZTYN. The Gothic High Gate in the Old Town.

OLSZTYN, the capital of the Varmia and Mazury region, boasts fine 18th-century tenement houses on the Old Town Market Square.

LIDZBARK WARMIŃSKI – from the mid 14th century this was the seat of the Bishops of Varmia. The Gothic-style Bishop's Palace has a square design.

LIDZBARK WARMIŃSKI. The Castle houses the Varmia Museum. These carvings are from a 15th-century altar at Trelkowo near Szczytno.

*LAKE DADAJ is not far from Biskupiec.
This is the typical landscape
of the Mazurian Lakeland.*

*ŚWIĘTA LIPKA boasts a Baroque Jesuit monastery
complex with the Church of the Visitation.
The interior of the latter has a famous organ with
moving decorative elements.*

*A folk group guards the traditions
of the Varmia-Mazury region.*

The SUWAŁKI REGION with its characteristic erratics (giant boulders dropped by melting glaciers at the end of the Ice Age).

STAŃCZYKI. Poland's tallest viaduct carrying a now-disused railway line.

The SUWAŁKI REGION is a picturesque land of elevations and deep-set lakes.

WIGRY. The Baroque-style post-Cameldolite monastery complex by Lake Wigry.

THE RIVER BIEBRZA
and its tributaries create
extensive floodlands in
spring. The National Park
established here protects rare
flora and fauna, as well as
the unique natural landscape
of the floodplain.

*CIECHANOWIEC boasts
the Outdoor Museum
of Agriculture with its examples
of peasant and manorial
buildings. This windmill was
brought here from a village
in Podlasie region.*

BIAŁYSTOK, on the River Biała,
was founded in the 15th century.
The Baroque palace and park complex of the
Branicki family has won itself the nickname
"the Versailles of Podlasie".

BIAŁYSTOK. Part of the interior
of the Branicki Palace.

BIAŁOWIEŻA. Tarpan-type horses at the National Park's Show Reserve.

BIAŁOWIEŻA NATIONAL PARK is of such importance to the world that UNESCO has recognised it as both a Biosphere Reserve and a World Heritage Site.

THE BIAŁOWIEŻA FOREST is a unique, pristine wilderness, whose greatest attraction is probably the European bison.

HAJNÓWKA. Poland's largest Orthodox place of worship is the new Church of the Holy Trinity.

GRABARKA is the most famous shrine of the Orthodox Church in Poland. These crosses of penitence were brought here by the faithful.

SIERPC. The Museum of the Mazovian Countryside brings together old farmsteads, chapels and farming implements on a 60 ha site.

CZERWIŃSK was once a centre of trade along the Vistula. It features a monastery of canons-regular with a Romanesque church.

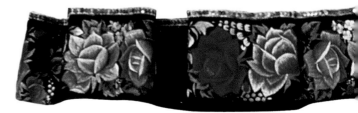

NIEBORÓW. *Set in extensive parkland, the 17th-century Baroque palace is one of the most valuable heritage buildings in the Mazowsze region.*

Łowicz folk costume characteristic of the Mazowsze region.

WARSAW is the capital of both Poland and the Mazowsze region. Almost completely destroyed during World War II, its rebuilding was an act of determination and self-belief. Today the city again features such fine views as this – of Castle Square with the Royal Castle and the Column of King Zygmunt III Vasa.

WARSAW. A portrait of King Zygmunt III Vasa in the Castle's Marble Room.

WARSAW. The Royal Castle's Marble Room with its portraits of Poland's Kings. In the middle is the likeness of King Stanisław August Poniatowski.

WARSAW. The Old Town Market Square with tenement houses rebuilt faithfully in their 17th-18th century forms.

WARSAW. The Barbican – the impressive fortification of the New Town Gate within the defensive walls of the Old Town.

WARSAW. The Mermaid of the Old Town is but one representation of this aquatic symbol of Warsaw, which features on the city's coat of arms.

WARSAW. The Łazienki Park and Palace complex with its neo-Classical Palace on the Island. This was the seat of Poland's last King, Stanisław August Poniatowski, who reigned until 1795.

WARSAW. The fifties-style Palace of Culture and Science has become its own unique kind of tourist attraction.

WARSAW. Wilanów, on the city's southern edge, boasts one of the finest magnate's residences in Poland. Here we see the front elevation of the palace, which was summer home to King Jan III Sobieski (reigning 1674-1696).

KAZIMIERZ DOLNY – a picturesque place of recreation by the Vistula – has a Renaissance-style architectural layout.

This is the Market Square with a view of the parish church.

KAZIMIERZ DOLNY. An element of the Renaissance facade to the Celejowska tenement house on Senatorska Street.

KAZIMIERZ DOLNY. The tenement house of the Przybył family, with its richly-decorated facade, dates back to 1615.

LUBLIN. The defensive Krakowska
Gate in the Gothic-Renaissance style.

LUBLIN. From the 12th century onwards this
was a fortified town devastated at regular intervals
by invaders from the east.

This facade is of the 14th-century castle rebuilt
in the neo-Gothic style at the beginning of the 19th century.

LUBLIN. A harvest wreath
in the Museum
of the Lublin Countryside.

NAŁĘCZÓW is a famous
spa with potable mineral
waters. The wooden
church is in the typical
style of the Podhale
region.

ZAMOŚĆ is a city with a unique Renaissance architectural layout and town plan.
The Mannerist-Baroque style Town Hall from the 17th century features a 52-metre tower and monumental 18th-century steps.

ZAMOŚĆ. 17th-century arcaded tenement houses on the Old Market Square recall the Renaissance architecture of Italy.

LEŻAJSK is on the edge of the Sandomierz Forest.
The 17th-century organ in the town's Bernardine church is one of Poland's finest.

JAROSŁAW is an old fortified town on the heights above the River San. The Market Square has a Town Hall that is now Neo-Renaissance in style.

PRZEMYŚL. Old tenement houses with arcades on the picturesque sloping Market Square.

KRASICZYN features the Renaissance-Mannerist castle of the Krasicki family set in a 19th-century landscaped park.

LAKE SOLIŃSKIE is a dam reservoir along the San – a place for water-based recreation and sport at the foot of the Bieszczady Mountains.

RZESZÓW. This 18th-century Late Baroque palace was a summer residence for the Lubomirski family.

RZESZÓW, a town on the Wisłok, was first settled in the Neolithic period. Here we see the Market Square with its eclectic-style Town Hall dating back to the 19th century.

RZESZÓW and the Castle of the Lubomirski family. This is a 19th-century construction built upon surviving fortifications from at least 200 years earlier.

SANDOMIERZ is a beautiful example of architectural and town planning. This photograph shows the Market Square with its Renaissance Town Hall.

ZALIPIE. The "Painted Village", where local tradition dictates that houses, other buildings and household equipment should all be painted.

BARANÓW SANDOMIERSKI boasts a Mannerist-style 16th-17th century castle with characteristic corner towers.

KRAKÓW is a historic city, and a centre of Polish culture and national identity. Here a bas-relief features the emblem of the city.

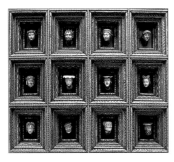

KRAKÓW. The Wawel Hill. The ceiling of the Chamber of Deputies, otherwise known as the "Under the Heads" Hall.

KRAKÓW. The Wawel Hill is a limestone height overlooking the Vistula. Its complex of historic buildings includes the Gothic--Renaissance Castle, the Gothic Cathedral (pictured here) and defensive ramparts.

KRAKÓW. The Main Market Square (Rynek Główny) with
the Clothiers' Hall and Gothic-style Church of the Virgin Mary.

The girl in Kraków
dress.

KRAKÓW. The Mariacki
Church has an
altar by Veit Stoss,
which was carved
in lime wood in
the 15th century.

OGRODZIENIEC. The ruins of the 16th-century Renaissance-style castle sit upon 504 m Castle Hill, the highest point in the Kraków-Częstochowa Upland.

MIRÓW. Ruins of the Gothic-style castle erected in the 14th century (the times of Kazimierz the Great).

THE KRAKÓW-CZĘSTOCHOWA UPLAND is a limestone plateau on which such rocks are a characteristic element of the landscape.

PIESKOWA SKAŁA is a limestone pinnacle c. 25 m high which gains it name from a characteristic shape said to recall that of the Club of Hercules.

THE ŁOKIETKA CAVE in Ojców has 270 m of subterranean passages and chambers lit by electric light. This is the so-called Knights' Hall (Sala Rycerska).

THE PIENINY MOUNTAINS are a small, but picturesque chain cut through by the River Dunajec.

NIEDZICA features a partially-ruined fort which gained itself a fine location when a reservoir filled behind the Czorsztyn dam.

DĘBNO PODHALAŃSKIE. The wooden Church of St. Michael the Archangel dates back to the second half of the 15th century.

A young raftsman in regional costume.

THE DUNAJEC has cut a series of beautiful gorges through the Pieniny Mountains. Rafting its fast-flowing waters has become a major tourist attrraction.

ZAKOPANE has been Poland's most famous resort since the 19th century. The characteristic silhouette of Giewont mountain towers above it.

PODHALE REGION. A colourful Corpus Christi procession.

A girl in Highland folk costume.

ZAKOPANE. The little chapel at Jaszczurówka was designed in the Zakopianski style established by Stanisław Witkiewicz.

ZAKOPANE. A bas-relief presents ferns, martagon lily and the stemless carline thistle, a favourite decorative element in the Podhale region.

THE TATRAS are the loftiest and most diverse massif in the Western Carpathians. The highest peak in the Polish part of the range is 2499 m Rysy. Here we see Mnich ("The Monk") above the mountain tarn known as Morskie Oko ("The Sea's Eye").

THE TATRA MOUNTAINS. A hiker on the mountain track. Chains and pegs are there to help him when the going gets tough.

THE TATRA MOUNTAINS. The chamois is a specific element of the area's fauna.

THE TATRA MOUNTAINS are a mecca for Polish skiers.
This is the Gąsienicowa Valley with the Granaty, Kozi Wierch, Zamarła Turnia
and Kościelec peaks.

THE TATRA MOUNTAINS. Carpets of crocuses bloom
in early spring in the Chochołowska Valley.

Nicolaus Copernicus (1473-1543)

Born in Toruń, Kopernik (as he is known in Poland) went on to study in Kraków and in Italy. A multitalented man of learning, he changed thinking on Earth's place in the universe with his heliocentric theory. His work De Revolutionibus Orbium Coelestium ("On the Revolution of the Celestial Spheres") thus laid the foundations of modern cosmology and influenced many branches of the then scientific world.

The Monument to Nicolaus Copernicus in Warsaw was designed by Bertel Thorvaldsen.

Tadeusz Kościuszko (1746-1817)

Jan III Sobieski (1629-1696)

King of Poland from 1674, he "won his spurs" in battle against the Swedes, the Tartar and Cosack armies and the Turks. His greatest feat of arms came in 1683, with the defeat of the Turkish army then besieging Vienna.

A portrait of King Jan III Sobieski from Wilanów in Warsaw.

A statue of King Jan III Sobieski by Warsaw's Łazienki Park. It was unveiled in 1788.

Kazimierz Pułaski (1747-1779)

Heading the armed forces during the so-called Kościuszko Rising of 1794, he defeated the Russian army at the Battle of Racławice. He had distinguished himself previously in the course of the American War of Independence, notably as a brigadier-general at the Battle of Saratoga in 1777.

The Monument to Tadeusz Kościuszko against the background of the tower of the Zymuntowska Cathedral on the Wawel Hill in Kraków.

Commander in the Bar Confederacy, and defender of Jasna Góra against the Russians, he commanded a cavalry brigade in George Washington's army during the American War of Independence. He died of wounds inflicted at the Battle of Savannah.

This Monument to Kazimierz Pułaski in Warka was unveiled in 1979.

Adam Mickiewicz (1798-1855)

Poland's greatest poet, or for Poles "The Bard", he spent most of his life as an exile, for longest in France. Co-creater of the Polish Romantic Movement, ideologist and independence activist, his artistic genius can be seen in his national epic Pan Tadeusz, amongst other places.

The Adam Mickiewicz Monument in Warsaw was funded by public contribution to mark the 100th anniversary of the author's birth.

The 18th-century palace of the Pułaski family is now the Kazimierz Pułaski Museum in Warka.

Fryderyk Chopin (1810-1849)

A portrait of Fryderyk Chopin to be seen at his Żelazowa Wola home.

Poland's most outstanding composer and pianist, and an icon of the Romantic era. Chopin's artistry was inspired by his country's folk music, and he composed a great many dance miniatures taking the form of waltzes, mazurkas and polonaises. His works are still among the most frequently performed. Warsaw plays host to the international piano competition held in his name every five years since 1927.

The Chopin Monument in Łazienki Park is the work of Wacław Szymanowski. Unveiled in 1926, it was deliberately destroyed during World War II, only to be faithfully reconstructed afterwards.

The first bars of Chopin's famous Polonaise in A major.

The manor house at Żelazowa Wola, the birthplace of Fryderyk Chopin, is now a museum to the famous composer. Chopin piano concerts are held here regularly.

Allegro con brio

Helena Modrzejewska (1840-1909)

Poland's greatest actress, who appeared in the United States from 1877 on, under the name Modjeska. She was to play 260 roles, including 35 in English and 17 of Shakespeare's characters. She was also considered one of the outstanding beauties of her age.

Helena Modrzejewska in a picture painted by Tadeusz Adjukiewicz.

Ignacy Jan Paderewski (1860-1941)

A bust of Ignacy Jan Paderewski at the Fryderyk Chopin Academy of Music in Warsaw.

Joseph Conrad (1857-1924) (Teodor Józef Konrad Korzeniowski)

Twenty years as a mariner left Conrad, who became a British citizen in 1886, one of the greatest of all writers of sea stories. Against such a background, he placed great emphasis on matters ethical, notably honour, duty, loyalty and moral rectitude. His best-known works include "Heart of Darkness", "Almayer's Folly" and "Lord Jim".

The monument to Józef Konrad Korzeniowski (Joseph Conrad) at the very edge of the sea in Gdynia.

The outstanding pianist, composer, politician and social activist whose efforts help lead to the rebirth of the Polish state. He signed the Treaty of Versailles in 1919 as Prime Minister and Foreign Secretary of his newly-reestablished country, and went on to represent it in the League of Nations.

Maria Skłodowska-Curie (1867-1934)

A great Polish physicist and chemist living in France and married (from 1895) to French physicist Pierre Curie. Together they discovered the elements radium and polonium in 1898 – an achievement for which they won the Nobel Prize for physics in 1903. The by-then-widowed Maria went on to win a second, for chemistry, in 1911.

The Monument to Maria Skłodowska-Curie on the small square by the Warsaw Centre for Oncology bearing her name. Pre-War this was known as the Radium Institute.

Karol Szymanowski (1882-1937)

The Atma Villa was the place of Karol Szymanowski's stays in Zakopane. It is now a museum devoted to the composer's life and works.

A Polish composer of the "Young Poland" period whose work involved the artistic stylization of Polish folk music, especially that of the Kurpie and Highland regions. His best-known works include the opera "Król (King) Roger" and the ballet "Harnasie".

Józef Piłsudski (1867-1935)

A great statesman who was Naczelnik ("Leader") and Marshal of Poland. In the years 1919-20, he successfully pursued a military campaign against the Russian bolsheviks, crowning the achievement with the 1921 Peace of Riga. Five years later he staged what became known as the "May Coup". He was twice Prime Minister of his country: in 1926-28 and in 1930.

The Monument to Marshal Józef Piłsudski stands by the Belvedere Palace next to Warsaw's Łazienki Park. It was unveiled in 1998.

John Paul II
(Karol Wojtyła)
(1920-2005)

Elected Pope in 1978, as the first non-Italian for 400 years. He was born in Wadowice, studied at universities in Kraków and Rome, and became Metropolitan Archbishop of Kraków in 1964. He was elevated to Cardinal in 1967. In the time that he was the Pope has made no fewer than 104 foreign pilgrimages.

The Polish Pope John Paul II, was the spiritual mainstay for his fellow countrymen and women in their years of struggle with the communist system, as well as in the subsequent period of transformation in post-1990 Poland. On May 1st 2011, the Pontiff joined the ranks of those declared "Blessed" by the Catholic Church.

A statue of John Paul II before the All Saints Church in Warsaw's Grzybowski Square.

Lech Wałęsa (born 1943)

Famed as a trade-union activist and politician, though an electrician by profession, Wałęsa rose to prominence as the unchallenged and unquestioned leader of Solidarity (*Solidarność*) – the independent trade union that emerged and grew between August 1980 and December 1981 into an independence-minded social movement of 10 million members. Things had all started with Wałęsa as one of the organisers of a localised strike at the Gdańsk Shipyard, but this and subsequent events are widely considered to have played a key role in the wave of democratic change that swept through the Eastern Bloc as a whole in the 1980s. The achievements (and what they promised) were such as to earn Wałęsa the 1983 Nobel Peace Prize. In the newly-democratic Poland of 1990, Lech Wałęsa was elected President, serving one full five-year term in that office.

On November 15th 1989, Lech Wałęsa gave his historic address before a joint session of both Houses of the US Congress.

Jerzy Owsiak in Gdańsk during the 16th (2008) Final of the "Great Orchestra of Holiday Help" (Wielka Orkiestra Świątecznej Pomocy) (Archive photo from WOŚP taken by Arek Drygas).

Jerzy Owsiak (born 1953)

Social activist, journalist, co-founder and President of the "Great Orchestra of Holiday Help" (*Wielka Orkiestra Świątecznej Pomocy*), which "played" for the first time in 1993. Telethon-like in structure, each year's *Orkiestra* collects money for the purchase of medical equipment capable of supporting the health and lives in children. By the end of the 2011 event, in excess of 140 million US dollars had been raised. The actions are followed and participated in enthusiastically by the Polish public each year, and this vast charitable undertaking does much to promote the good name of Poland far and wide. Owsiak's Foundation is also behind rock concerts under the *Przystanek Woodstock* title, bringing young people together in the name of "Love, Friendship and Music", as well as commitments to eschew violence and narcotics.